Juicing for Jocks

**AN
ATHLETE'S GUIDE TO FRESH JUICING
FOR PEAK PERFORMANCE**

BY JOAN STANEK

JUICING
FOR JOCKS

To my brother Kevin McGloin.

You have always been a shining light for our family.
May the road always rise to meet you and may the Commodores
be there to greet you. Thank you for your contribution to
my life and to this book.

Library of Congress Control Number: 2004099175

ISBN: 0976222108

Juicing for Jocks, LLC conducts seminars to discuss the positive impact fresh juicing can have on young athletes. To find out how a seminar can be conducted for your school, team or organization, please visit our Web site at www.juicingforjocks.com or email us at info@juicingforjocks.com.

Book Design: Andrew Rogers, Joslin Lake Design, www.joslinlakedesign.com
Editor: Riva Hemond, 1613786 Ontario LTD., riva@hemond.com

CONTENTS

Health and wellness are my passions, but athletes are my inspiration!

INTRODUCTION

Health and wellness are my passions, but athletes are my inspiration! One of my other passions in life is my position as Human Resources Director at a market-making firm by the name of Wolverine Trading, LLC, in downtown Chicago. It's a wonderful thing to be surrounded each day by such youth and vitality. I realized early on in my career that I had better listen to young people because I could definitely learn from them. They have a full day of very challenging work and still find time to stay connected to their health by working out, watching what they eat and participating in competitive sports.

Katie Gallagher, Equity Trader for Wolverine Trading, shared a story with me about one of the traders in her pit at the Chicago Board Options Exchange who had overcome the daily health hazards of trading by engaging in a daily ritual of juicing. Carrot juice with apples was his drink of choice and he joked about his health being extra-ordinary but his hands turning orange. I can now confirm that he made up the "orange hands" part of that story. For those of you who have never visited the trading floors—the space is very limited and the number of people is easily in the thousands. Traders are very dedicated people and they show up to trade—rain or shine, sick or tired—even sick *and* tired. It is not unusual for colds and flu to be going around the trading floor all year long. This trader was onto something and I wanted to find out more about it.

I was intrigued by this new health phenomenon and chose to do some research on this whole "juicing" thing. I started out slow, but from that point on, my whole life changed. As the weeks went by I could physically feel the impact the daily juicing was having on my life and I felt alive. It made sense that I was feeling such aliveness because the juice produced "enzymes"

3

that remained alive for consumption—unlike store bought products that kill off these healthy enzymes in order to preserve shelf life. I was drinking life right into my body and it was responding. A few short months later, Wolverine Trading purchased a high-powered commercial juicer for the employees and it has really made a difference. Some mornings we cannot keep up with all the juice requests!

My family became very curious. They began making inquiries into this mysterious lifestyle that I had become obsessed with. Our family soon invested in a high-powered juicer, which has since earned a permanent place on the kitchen counter. I began getting up earlier than usual to prepare the juice for everyone. I would deliver it right up to their rooms so that, with such great room service, there was no way they could refuse. My family implies that I actually "forced" the juice on them but that is not the way that I remember it at all.

My husband, Steve, and I soon began taking turns making the juice in the morning for all of us. It took as long to make as an average breakfast, but it was worth the time and energy once we began to experience the health benefits. Our children reported more energy and alertness in class after they began drinking the juice in the morning instead of eating a heavy breakfast. I no longer worried or felt guilty about not making a big, hot breakfast for them. As long as they were drinking the juices in the morning they were getting everything they needed. The benefits of the new breakfast routine were also confirmed by the fact that no one in the house was getting colds or flus anymore.

The juicing routine caught on quickly in our house especially during the summer months when dehydration was at its peak. My son, also named Steven, has played sports practically his whole life and was surprised by his body's response to the juicing. He sustained his strength and energy during practices for the hockey and football teams of Mount Carmel High

4

School in Chicago. He witnessed several fellow athletes collapsing during the strenuous practices due to dehydration and fatigue. I became more and more concerned with the health of my son and other young athletes who engage in strenuous and competitive sports. It is with this thought in mind that I was driven to find an answer to keeping our athletes on the ice, on the field or on the court!

We were surprised at how quickly our children adjusted to the morning juicing ritual and they began requesting "Carrots and Apples" only please! Our college-age daughter, Christin, realized that carrot juice was a quick cure for hangovers. Also, the allergies and stuffy noses that once plagued our home seemed to disappear as juicing became our weekday breakfast instead of eggs, toast and sausage. It fit in nicely with our busy schedule of being on the run and never having enough time to prepare a healthy meal. Most of the time, our children would take their juice with them in a "to-go" cup.

Our family still enjoys the many traditional meals that taste superb but lack proper nutritional value. The juicing lifestyle offsets some of the damage that we do to our bodies by consuming processed and fast foods. Juicing keeps sickness at bay and energizes our bodies on a daily basis.

I hope you enjoy this book. Believe me — it *will* make a difference in the lives of you and your children.

Joan Stonek

p.s.: JOCKS RULE!

1

WHAT I KNOW & LEARNED ABOUT
Juicing

I remember my parents saying, "*If I knew then what I know now, I'd be...*" Well now that I am in my early forties and my children are nearly independent, I think back to when they were young and we were constantly battling runny noses, sore throats, coughs, ear infections, stomachaches and fevers. I didn't realize the effect that food, specifically, processed food, had on their health. Back then, I didn't know anything about fresh juicing or its benefits. Vegetables were always cooked or steamed, so we were not receiving their full nutritional value. Our children received an adequate amount of sleep, three square meals a day and of course junk snacks but no soda. My mother-in-law suggested that, instead of Kool-Aid® or juices, to serve Jell-O® water, which was a mixture of gelatin powder and water. It had a nice color and the kids really enjoyed it. To this day, I attribute their good nails and hair to her suggestion.

It is very possible that had we introduced juicing into our lives when our children were very young, it

7

would have had a positive impact on our day-to-day health. We might have experienced fewer colds and viruses. Also, the introduction to juicing would have been easier; young children are so much more open. Carrot juice served in a cartoon character cup might have been an exciting adventure. The presentation of a meal or drink can determine whether or not we decide to sample it.

As our children got older their activities increased. It was a constant battle to keep them well enough so they would not miss practices and a chance to play the scheduled games or participate in the season's tournaments. I didn't realize at the time that their sicknesses might have been brought on by dehydration and processed food consumption. We were a pretty busy family—juggling jobs, chores and the kids' activities. Meals were sometimes put together with little or no preparation to keep up with the day's hectic schedule. I don't even want to think about the number of times I drove up to a window to get my kids dinner because we were running late for some activity. The next time you drive by any fast food restaurant, just count the number of mini-vans filled with kids—you will be shocked and amazed. Don't lose hope yet.

There is another way and I will show you.

When our kids got sick, we took them to the pediatrician. The doctor would diagnose whatever illness was being passed around at school that week and prescribe an antibiotic or over-the-counter medicine, which was taken until the sickness subsided. It usually took forever until they felt 100 percent. Daily juicing could have prevented some or all of these illnesses. Juicing builds the immune system so that the body can fight off symptoms of illness. We need to take a more proactive approach in preventing sickness in our children, and juicing is a way that we can accomplish this. People often take daily vitamins to prevent illness. Vitamins do help, but the benefits are not realized until

they reach the stomach. The benefit of juicing is imme-
diate because the digestive process begins in the mouth.

Food is key. It is really all about the food. Eighty-
percent of the food we eat is processed. Most of us do
not eat a diet of raw foods—and if we do, we cannot eat
enough to make a difference. We are not farm animals
that can consume mass quantities of raw vegetables
and get the benefits. Cows don't eat meat—only raw
vegetables and look how strong they are. What we put
in our bodies will determine our energy level and our
quality of life. Like most things in life; the better the
quality, the longer it will last and the more value we
get out of it. Raw foods are almost always good quality.
Raw equals life.

A raw foods and juicing lifestyle has a powerful
healing effect on people, especially those in chronically
poor health. Suddenly the body is getting the proteins,
vitamins, nutrients and hydration it craves… and it
likes it! In turn, the body thanks you by responding
with an improved and enhanced appearance, higher
energy and endurance levels, and an overall feeling of
new life and clarity.

ALKALINE BODY VS. ACIDIC BODY

Our body will function at its best in an "alkaline" state
vs. an "acidic" state. Your body's balance will depend upon
your diet and the amount of foods that you consume
that produce either "alkaline" results or "acidic" results.
Cancer and disease cannot survive and reproduce in
a body that is mostly alkaline. To the contrary, cancer
and disease love to live inside of a body that is acidic.
It latches itself onto vital organs and weakens the
immune system, leaving the body susceptible to all
sorts of ailments and unhealthy conditions.

The acid-producing foods on the list (*sidebar*)
often include artificial sweeteners and other processed
chemicals. To create a more "alkaline" body environment,

**ACID-
PRODUCING
FOODS:**

Breads
Coffee
Dairy products
Eggs
Meat
Soft drinks
Sugar
Sweets
White flour

9

GREEN KAMUT CAN BE
ORDERED ONLINE AT
WWW.LIFESVIGOR.COM

you want to increase your consumption of raw fruits and vegetables. In addition, green food products such as "green kamut" and fresh juices help to create a balance in the body.

Certain foods that are acidic trigger the body to go into survival mode, which means extracting calcium and other minerals from the bones to neutralize all the acids in the system. This makes the body less efficient when it comes to absorption and assimilation of the "good stuff" that we consume. It is important to create a balanced environment of acid and alkaline. During times of sickness, there is often an imbalance of internal systems.

It is important to note that if the body is experiencing poor assimilation, it may not get the benefits of any vitamin supplements.

One way to check your body's pH balance is to purchase pH Test Strips. They can be found at most health food stores or whole food markets. A neutral pH balance is 7.0; considered healthy for most people. Test your child's pH balance and see if it changes with a diet of fresh juicing and raw foods.*

*
FOOTNOTES:
INFORMATION TAKEN
FROM THE FOLLOWING
WEB SITES:

WWW.WILDERNESS
FAMILYNATURALS.
COM

WWW.NATURAL
HEALTHSCHOOL.
COM

ENZYMES

Enzymes are important for a healthy, strong body. They assist us in our digestive process and help rebuild our bodies. The body loses enzymes by poor diet and insufficient consumption of raw fruits and vegetables as part of our daily diet. As our enzyme supply in our body is depleted, we begin to experience poor digestion and health problems. By the age of forty, only 30 percent of our original enzyme supply remains.

At birth we are given a certain number of enzymes for our lifetime. We cannot regenerate additional enzymes, but with a diet of fresh juicing or raw food, we will not deplete our supply of enzymes and we will continue to benefit from high energy, healthy skin,

10

weight maintenance, blood pressure regulation and overall health and vitality.

Juice is food and in its natural form—the body easily digests it. This makes a big difference to people who are ill and have digestive problems. The young who are very active need the nutrients from juicing to sustain their physical well being. The elderly, who have slowed down, and do not consume as much food but still need nutrients can truly benefit from juicing. Juicing can make a difference to everyone—from a rather healthy person, to the pregnant woman who is experiencing constant morning sickness, to someone who suffers from certain food allergies, to a cancer patient. Researchers estimate that 80 to 90 percent of all cancers are environmentally related.*

*
FOOTNOTE:
The Juice Lady's Guide to Juicing for Health,
CHERIE CALBOM, MS.,
1999, PAGE 60.

A juicing lifestyle improves and enhances all aspects of your physical being, from levels of energy to appearance.

11

2

WHY JUICING IS FOR

Jocks

ike most young parents, my husband and
I signed our children up for every sport
imaginable. We wanted to expose them to
all sorts of activities allowing them to
determine their sport of choice.

Our daughter Christin played soccer,
participated in theater and dance and went on to join the
crew team in high school and college. Steven, our son,
has been on a field, a court or the ice most of his life.
When he was about seven years old he played many
different sports. This trend lasted until he reached high
school when he participated in football and ice hockey.

It was during his high school years that I found
my voice and passion. I focused on finding a way to
improve the lives of young athletes. I realized that some
of the children participating in sports at a very young
age might not have a future on high school teams due
to health issues. Allergies, weaknesses, and viruses may
preclude them from participating in sports at a team
or recreational level. In other words—being unhealthy

13

"takes them out of the game." As you may know, once the pattern of sickness begins to develop in a young child, it's very difficult to keep him or her healthy and strong as their immune system becomes stressed and weak. Juicing can help strengthen a child's health and resistance to illnesses. Most doctors are unfamiliar and often unaware of the benefits of juicing. My information comes from my research and the experiences of my family and friends. At the start, I had to be open to trying something "new" and I am grateful that I was willing to put aside my tendency to grab the "easy fix." A child or an athlete that is healthy and strong can look forward to a future filled with challenge and competition. A juicing lifestyle provides the groundwork for increased endurance and a higher level of performance.

An athlete will perform better if his or her body is hydrated and filled with nutrients. My son endured hours of training and conditioning for high school football during the long, hot summer months and he was never taken out of the game by sickness.

Let's face it—as a society of adults, teenagers and children, we are not going to give up fast food and a convenient life style. This book does not propose you do so. Rather, it suggests that the inclusion of raw foods, in the form of juicing, into your family's daily life can make a significant difference; especially in active children and teenagers.

Sports activities require that kids be healthy. Ask yourself how many times you have wanted to keep your kids at home from a sport activity due to a flu or cold. How much better would their experience have been if they had been feeling strong and healthy?

Our children have experienced the benefits of juicing first hand. Their bodies now indicate to them very clearly when they have been neglecting their juicing routine and eating too many processed foods. Their symptoms include loss of energy, upset stomachs, feeling of bloatedness and weakness.

14

Processed foods are anything that is not raw in its natural form. Raw foods and juicing have a common factor—they are still in their natural form, which means they have not been altered in anyway. Most of the foods that we buy in the store or prepare at home have been altered in some way. They have been processed with preservatives and chemicals to extend shelf life and improve appearance. When eaten, the body needs to work very hard at breaking down the preservatives and chemicals contained in these foods. The body must figure out what to use and what to store. For the most part, the body ends up storing most of the processed foods that we consume because it is unable to utilize most of it. In the case of raw foods and juicing, the body uses less energy to break down food and digest it because the body assimilates the food better when in its natural form. It uses more and stores less. This is one reason why weight control is so easy for juicers and raw foodists because of the food assimilation factor.

Another important aspect of fresh juicing is the "enzyme factor." Fresh juicing produces "live enzymes" that are living molecules that our bodies need and crave to sustain optimum health and vitality.

Store-bought fruit and vegetable juices no longer have these enzymes. They are killed off in the manufacturing process; therefore the juice has little or no nutritional value. The packaging can be very alluring, but don't be fooled—it is merely a sugar rush with some Vitamin C thrown in for good measure.

Once you have prepared your juice, drink it as soon as possible to get the full benefit of the "live enzymes" for your body. We usually drink our juice in the morning while we are getting ready for the day or take it in a to-go cup if we are running late.

Juicing requires a small monetary investment and a little of your time. The only monetary investment is the purchase of a good juice extraction machine. The time investment involves getting out to buy fresh fruits and

The inclusion of raw foods in the form of juicing into your family's daily life can make a difference; especially in active children and teenagers.

15

vegetables, and then a few minutes each day to prepare the juice. Soon you will realize that it was worth the investment. Your body will thank you in the form of fresh looking skin, a higher level of energy and an overall feeling of wellness.

During my juicing research, I remembered a key point that made complete sense to me; any vegetable that comes from the ground had to have oxygen in order to grow. By ingesting these vegetables we are in essence breathing oxygen and life right into our bodies. It is the difference between putting something that is "alive" into your body or something that is "dead". Your body will feel and look better after juicing. When your diet consists of more processed food than raw fruits and vegetables, you will not perform as well or look as good as you should or want.

BENEFITS OF JUICING

Replaces a meal (helps wrestlers and football players who are trying to hydrate their bodies but maintain weigh-in)

Easy to digest—doesn't exhaust the body

Hydrates the body and feeds the muscles

Increases energy and endurance level

Contains "live" enzymes which feed all the cells in your body. By drinking something that is alive —you will feel and look vibrant!

TIPS FOR PARENTS & COACHES

Don't try to get your kids or your players to try juicing if you are not willing to do it also.

The process is fun and easy, so allow the kids to make their own juices. They will begin to come up with their own concoctions.

Once or twice a week allow them to have the choice of having juice for dinner instead of a cooked meal. If they are picky eaters, they may be getting so many more nutrients from the juice than the food they're not eating.

Coaches may want to require the players to juice before and after practice for endurance and weight maintenance. You will be surprised at your player's level of performance and endurance at practices and games.

Replace sugary and rich deserts with fruit smoothies.

Have a "salad bar night" for dinner once a week and allow them to invite a friend to share this new dinner experience. They can make up their own salads with all the fixings.

Always send them to bed with a glass of water for thirst during the night and upon waking in the morning. Water in the morning is a great start to the day!

Stop buying soft drinks and store bought juices which contain corn syrup. Corn syrup is not natural and may be linked to obesity in adults and children. It is cheaper to manufacture than using real sugar and is contained in almost all processed foods.* Serve fresh juices and encourage more water consumption with meals and in-between.

Juicing is a "quick fix" so you can go about your day feeling energized.

*
FOOTNOTE:
REFERENCE ON
CORN SYRUP:

"THE DEVIL'S CANDY",
SUSAN KLEINER, PhD

WWW.MENSHEALTH.
COM/FEATURES

SEARCH UNDER
"HEALTH"

17

3

CHILDHOOD Ailments

My children experienced some of the ailments mentioned in the sidebar to the right. It's possible had I known then what I know now about juicing, they may have been sick less, missed fewer school days and been more active in their daily lives.

You want the best quality of life for you and your children and that means the best health. This can be achieved at *any* age by "juicing."

Short juice fasts for a day or two can be beneficial and can accelerate the healing process. They offer the body a chance to rest from digestive activity and instead concentrate on fighting infection. The aliveness of the raw juices supports the body in the healing process. Over-the-counter medicines do not help healing or reduce the duration of the illness, but rather treat the symptoms. I would recommend that you educate yourself regarding the process of juice fasting. Several books are available and they can be quite beneficial to the health

FRESH JUICING MAY IMPROVE AILMENTS SUCH AS:

Acne
Allergies
Asthma
Colds
Dehydration
Juvenile Diabetes
Obesity

19

of your family and especially your young athletes. (*Resources for health and wellness can be found in Chapter 8*). Following are some typical illnesses, along with examples of the beneficial transformations realized by people who have incorporated juicing into their daily lives.

ASTHMA

Asthma is a chronic disease that affects millions of children, many from birth. Some children are fortunate and grow out of it, but most are not and suffer with this

ailment throughout their lives. Asthma robs children of their ability to enjoy a healthy life and makes sports participation risky.

An acquaintance of mine told me about her experience with asthma and how it plagued her until high school. Due to the asthma, she could not follow her dream and swim competitively. She spoke with her medical doctor and chiropractor and together they came up with a daily nutritional diet that was mainly juicing. The juicing changed her life. She became strong and well enough to swim competitively in high school. Today, at 40 years of age, she owes her strength and well-being to a juicing and raw food diet.

Currently, I am employed at a firm that has a full-service kitchen for its employees. The chef, Joe Gomez, used to eat a typical Midwestern diet — red meat, chicken and lots of starches. He and his family consumed little or no vegetables or raw food. Since

20

childhood, he suffered from chronic asthma, sleep apnea and weight gain.

Due to my nagging, he began reading about the health benefits of juicing and soon began "fresh juicing" each day. He started with a 21-day juice fast, which meant not eating any solid food for 21 days. He had a wonderful experience with the juice fast and was amazed at how his body reacted to this new process. Following the juice fast, he continued juicing throughout the day (two–three times per day) and incorporated only raw foods (fruits and vegetables) into his daily diet. Within the first 30 days, he could feel a significant difference in his breathing and physical well-being. A year later, he went to his asthma doctor, who has treated him since he was a child; the doctors and nurses were amazed at his test results. He showed no signs of asthma. He told the doctor that he no longer needed the prescription and that he would be running in the Chicago Marathon. In addition, he said farewell to the sleep apnea apparatus that he had to use in order to get rest each night.

Joe Gomez is an example and an inspiration to young and old who suffer from sicknesses such as asthma and sleep apnea. He is someone who was courageous enough to take control of his life and his health. It was not enough that he wanted to be well—he knew that he had to do something about it.

The following juices can be helpful in relieving the symptoms of asthma in children:

- Onion Juice — *Discards mucus in the upper respiratory tract.*

- Parsley Juice — *No more than one cup per day. Note: can be toxic in overdose, especially pregnant women.*

- Radish Juice

- Carrot Juice

21

ALLERGIES

All of us have experienced some form of allergies during our lifetime affecting our skin, nasal passages or our respiratory tract.

Most of the time we are able to fight off or rid ourselves of the symptoms within a short period of time with various types of treatments. Unfortunately for some children and young teens, allergies can interfere with leading a productive life.

Most allergy symptoms are brought on by food consumption. This is due in part to the excessive food additives and flavorings that are contained in all processed foods. You can strengthen the immune system and ward off the reactions to these chemical additives by consuming more raw fruits and vegetables and "fresh juice."

The following juices are recommended:

- Celery Juice — *Helps to reduce allergic reactions.*
- Parsley Juice — *Helps stop hay fever attacks.*
  Note: can be toxic in overdose, especially pregnant women.
- Carrot Juice — *Good for everything.*

COLDS

When our children were young, coughs, fevers and runny noses were a way of life. We always kept a supply of various cough medicines and decongestants on hand to relieve the symptoms. Juicing would have made a huge difference in our children's health and well-being.

Since medicine does not build up our children's immunity, we, as parents, should take a more active role in building up our children's bodies and systems to protect them against these childhood ailments and diseases. It is a great source of comfort to know that we have the medicine available if our children need it, but it is far better to take a more proactive and preventative role. Years ago, at the first sign of a sniffle or fever we would immediately begin giving our children some sort of over-the-counter fever reducer or decongestant because we wanted to prevent the sickness from getting worse. If the sickness progressed, it would mean an unscheduled day off of work, school, and sports practice, which could eliminate an athlete from an upcoming game. Now, we all know what kind of stress that causes the family. For years, I didn't realize that I was only treating the symptoms and not the actual sickness. The symptoms are actually the body's natural way of healing and ridding itself of something that does not belong. When the body is bombarded with all sorts of various medicines, we end up just confusing our immune system—and the healing process stops. Eating heavily-processed foods while sick with fevers, colds and congestion further delays the healing process. The body is unable to heal and digest food simultaneously; therefore if the body is healing and food is ingested, the healing process will stop to begin digesting food. It would explain why colds and congestion take forever to go away. Some adults and children suffer from these symptoms all year round—unable to free themselves from the discomfort.

Fresh juicing for a day or so can actually expedite the healing process and allow the body the time and rest needed from food digestion to rid the body of sickness. When on a juice fast, it is recommended that you stay indoors and rest and keep your activities to a minimum. If you are interested in learning more about "juice fasting" or "detoxing," please refer to *Detox Your World* by Shazzie, published by Raw Creation, Ltd.

If you or your family suffers from chronic sickness, you may want to read the book, *Raw Family: A True Story of Awakening* by Victoria Boutenko. She was inspired to write the book after her family's experience with sickness and how their lives changed after being introduced to juicing and raw foods, which would include raw fruits and vegetables. Every parent should read this book.

You want the best quality of life for you and your children and that means the best health. This can be achieved at *any* age by "juicing."

23

ACNE

The lymphatic system (the skin) is the biggest organ in the body. Toxins make their way in and out of this organ each and every day at lightning speed. If your child suffers from either a mild or severe case of acne, a daily diet of fresh juicing could make a world of difference for their body and their skin.

Acne is a sign from your body that something is wrong. Toxins are being blocked, and since they cannot make their way out through the particular organ, the skin is the next viable exit. Treating acne with such medications as antibiotics can definitely show improvement but you are exposing your child to other health risks.

Internal cleansing programs that are administered by trained technicians can be beneficial in cleansing the body of unwanted toxins. For instance, "colonics" are a historical method that is now becoming more popular for cleansing the colon. Most disease and sickness begins in the colon. Years ago, people would attempt to heal themselves from fevers and other types of sickness by giving themselves enemas. It is not a very popular subject to discuss, but is a very authentic and natural way to rid the body of unwanted toxins that can lead to sickness. Unfortunately, we live in a society that supports the idea of a "quick fix" with various medications that only treat the symptoms. That may be why the same cold or flu tends to show up again in a month or so.

Karyn Calabrese, owner and operator of Karyn's Inner Beauty Center in Chicago (www.karynraw.com), says that we are a society who is "dying for convenience." She is so right. We don't care what drive-thru foods are doing to our bodies or those of our children as long as we get our quick fix so we can get to the next task at hand. We would rather tolerate sickness and weakness brought on by processed food consumption than think about changing our relationship to food and the way

We would rather tolerate sickness and weakness brought on by processed food consumption than change our relationship to those foods.

24

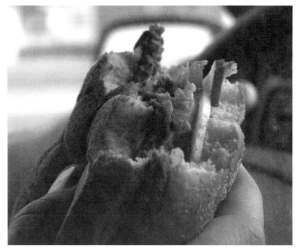

we eat and feed our families. Many people are intolerant to dairy products and take a pill (which also have side affects) in order to be able to eat their favorite foods. The idea that "maybe" they should eliminate dairy does not seem to be an option they would consider. Intolerance to dairy is an indication that your body does not want it. We often dismiss these messages and continue to eat things that "we like" but are not necessarily what our body wants and needs for well-being. Until we make the correct nutritional choices, sickness will always be a part of our lives.

Introducing juicing in the morning for breakfast and the evening as a snack or in place of dinner will definitely improve acne. It will begin to hydrate the cells in the body and will improve the skin. Severe cases may warrant additional steps. I would recommend a cleansing program and/or detox first.

The following juices are recommended for acne suffers:

- → Carrots, celery and cucumber
- → Carrots, celery and parsley
- → Celery, fresh spinach, cucumber, parsley

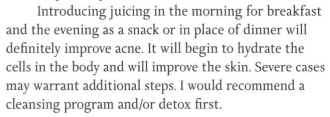

Cramps
**Dry lips and
mouth**
Fatigue
Flushed skin
Headache
Irritability
**Stiff and/or
painful joints**
**Urine begins
to darken
and output
decreases**

*

DEHYDRATION

*"Dehydration is the condition that results when too much body fluid is lost."**

If your child is telling you that he or she is thirsty, then the child is already dehydrated. We don't always pay attention to the signs that our bodies give us (*see sidebar*).

Most athletes experience dehydration at one time or another. It is important to treat the symptoms of dehydration *immediately* so it does not become severe. Serious cases can lead to weak, rapid heartbeat and low blood pressure, which can lead to shock and death.

Keeping the body hydrated throughout the day is the best practice. Athletes should always carry around a bottle of water or Rejuvelac and drink it even when they are not thirsty. Rejuvelac is a drink that you can make yourself at home. It helps clean the intestinal tract by loosening mucus and it is good for combating the effects of stress.** It contains protein, enzymes, and vitamin B-12. Eight glasses of water a day are recommended to keep the body well hydrated. Juicing in the morning and in the evening, along with daily intake of water, is the best source of hydration for a young athlete's body. It will sustain body fluids throughout the day during all those practices and games.

This can't be stressed enough—**hydration is extremely important**. Get your kids in the habit of drinking water all day long. If you need to, buy them an attractive water bottle and have them carry it in their book bags or on their bikes. Also, always leave a water bottle with fresh filtered water by their bed at night, so if they wake up thirsty they will have an ample supply. In the morning, give them some water to start out their day. You can add a small piece of fruit to brighten it up.

For times of vomiting and diarrhea, which can lead to dehydration and a slower healing process, a daily regime of juicing will offset some of the symptoms.

*
INFORMATION TAKEN
FROM:

HEALTH.DISCOVERY.
COM/DISEASESAND-
COND/ENCYCLOPEDIA/
591.HTML

**
SOURCE:

WWW.KARYNRAW.COM

Rejuvelac

Recipe from Ann Wigmore, Institute Kitchen. Mary Forest Finnell, ND, MH, LMT.

2 cups soft wheat berries
3 cups filtered water
*Note: You can find wheat berries at a raw food
store, or online at www.living-foods.com*

In order to make Rejuvelac, you will need to soak and sprout the
wheat berries. Seeds, grains and beans are filled with vital nutrients
but in their unsoaked form, they are very hard to eat and digest.
Sprouting not only brings forth the nutrients but also eliminates
certain acids and toxins in plant life that would otherwise interfere
with our digestion.

Soak the wheat berries in filtered water for 8 hours, or overnight.
You may stir once or twice with clean hands to activate the sprouting
process.

Drain and rinse the wheat berries and let sit in a jar or bowl for
two days—rinsing each day. After two days when white sprout tails
begin to show, add 6 cups filtered water, cover the jar with cheese
cloth, and put in a warm place where it can be exposed to at least
70°F temperature for two more days.

After two days, separate the water from the seeds. The liquid is
your Rejuvelac. You may drink it, refrigerate it, or use it in recipes.
The leftover seeds may be reused to make another batch—add 4
cups of filtered water, and soak for one day only. The seeds can then
be discarded outdoors as bird feed.

When refrigerated, Rejuvelac lasts two weeks.

Serves 12 (makes 3 cups)

27

OBESITY

Childhood obesity is an epidemic in the United States and in many countries around the world. More than 60 percent of Americans are overweight and about 30 percent are obese. Obesity plays a part in heart disease, diabetes, cancer and arthritis and in some cases death. The U.S. Medicare system recently declared that obesity should be labeled as a medical disease and therefore certain treatments and procedures associated with this illness will be covered by insurance.*

My recommendation for children who suffer from obesity is to enroll them in a detox program that involves a regime of juice fasting. A trained nutritionist or a raw food specialist should administer this process. (*See Chapter 8 for detox specialists sources.*)

A supervised detox program can jump-start a child's program of wellness. It is important to internally cleanse the body first, so the positive effects of juicing and a raw food diet will be assimilated completely and thoroughly. Most of what we consume is processed food and the body does not really use it—rather it stores most of it as fat or toxins. Over time, the fat/toxins

*

Source:

"Medicare redefines obesity as medical; change could allow coverage of treatment", Elizabeth Weise, *USA Today*, July 16, 2004, page A.01

overwhelm the body and create some illness in our children. When sickness occurs, we are mystified by its sudden appearance. What we don't realize is that illness does not happen suddenly; rather it takes time to build up. The body does a great job of trying to break down all the chemicals and processed food, but as extraordinary as the body is, it may not be able to sustain health for long periods of time.

After a detox, the body is much more receptive to the benefits of juicing and raw foods. It will be able to use these resources of nutrition in a whole new way and not store as many toxins. Ultimately, this will lead to a loss of weight and bloatedness and an increase in energy and vitality.

Detox has been used for quite sometime as a method of healing and there are several books and reference materials available to learn more about this process for all sorts of disease and illness especially for our young children. (*See Chapter 8 for detox sources.*)

Less weight and bloatedness is vitally important for an athlete who is actively participating in sports.

The following juice combinations are recommended for safe weight loss in children, and can be used in place of a meal:

➼ Carrot, cucumber and parsley—*Nourishes, hydrates, relieves bloatedness.*

➼ Carrot, celery and beet—*Hydrates, calms and flushes liver*

29

JUVENILE DIABETES

If your child has been diagnosed with juvenile diabetes, you must read the book written by Victoria Boutenko entitled, *Raw Family: A True Story of Awakening.* It is a wonderful, educational and inspiring story of how she totally healed her entire family of sickness in a period of one year by juicing and a raw food diet. Her youngest and only son had been diagnosed at the age of nine years old with juvenile diabetes. The doctors told her that he would probably require insulin his whole life. Ms. Boutenko didn't feel right about putting her son on the insulin due to its side effects. Through her research, she learned that it is not the actual diabetes that causes blindness and kidney failure but rather the insulin. After additional research about how people become healthy, she came upon the juicing and the raw food diet. Within six months, her family's health was totally turned around. They not only looked different but they felt amazing. Her son never needed to go on the insulin and he no longer has diabetes. He and his sister went on to write their own story for teenagers about raw food and how it changed their lives forever! The book is called *Eating Without Heating,* by Sergei and Valya Boutenko.

The following juice combinations can be helpful in relieving the symptoms of diabetes: *

➔ Cucumber, lemon and parsley—*Hydrates, flushes, diuretic*

➔ Romaine lettuce, celery, cucumber—*Low in sugar, high in nutrients*

----

*
FOOTNOTE:
INFORMATION
ON THE JUICE
RECOMMENDATIONS
AND COMBINATIONS
WAS TAKEN FROM:

The Juice Lady's Guide to Juicing for Health, CHERIE CALBOM, MS., 1999.

30

JOCKS RULE!

The information included in this chapter was just a sampling of the sickness and disease that families experience in raising children. Hopefully, this chapter opened your eyes to new methods of reducing or eliminating some of these conditions in your children.

Our young athletes take a chance everyday by getting out there and participating in sports. Why don't we meet them half way and take a chance on something new that could actually prolong and improve their childhood experience of playing sports!

4

GETTING Started

If you've gotten this far into the book, it can only mean you are interested in this concept and you believe it can make a difference for you and your family. Compliment yourself. It's a sure sign you care about your family's health and are willing to try something new. Like any change in habit, it will seem difficult and uncomfortable at first—but stick with it. I promise you will see positive changes!

Unfortunately, there will never be juice bars on every corner like there are fast food restaurants—but that doesn't mean healthy alternatives are to be overlooked. Our family lifestyle was probably very much like yours. Both parents working; very involved in the kids' school, sports and social activities; not much time for anything else. The number one question each day was what to do for dinner. "How can I possibly prepare a meal between today's events? I'll have to prepare something a day ahead." That usually never happened.

But I promise: you *can* fit this into your busy lifestyle. With the following paragraphs, I will give you

33

steps and helpful hints to get you started. By reading the book and accepting the concept, you've done the hard work—now here's the easy part:

STEP ONE—PURCHASE A JUICER

Research juice extractors on the Internet. You should expect to pay about $100.00. I recommend the **Jack LeLanne Power Juicer** or the **Juice Lady Pro JL500** juicer. Both have powerful motors, stainless steel parts, are easy to clean, and produce flavorful juices. And keep an eye open for our **Juicing for Jocks** juicer—hitting the market soon!

STEP TWO—START JUICING!

Start off with a simple juice combination of carrots and apples. Drink it for a short while and then begin adding other vegetables such as celery, spinach, romaine lettuce and beets in any combination.

The keys to successful juicing are using a good juicer and organic produce. The next chapter will provide you with specific recipes, but please have fun experimenting and creating your own combinations.

For more detailed recipes and descriptions to the benefits of the ingredients or combinations, please reference *The Juice Lady's Guide to Juicing for Health*, by Cherie Calbom, MS. Ms. Calbom gives very detailed information on healing illnesses with specific juice recipes. This book has been a great resource for me and I have given it to my friends and family.

STEP THREE—HELPFUL TIPS

🏃 Always try to buy certified organic fruits and vegetables. Most local supermarkets have an organic section, so it is easier than ever to get good-quality, pesticide-free produce for juicing.

34

Always wash your fruits and vegetables. If organic produce is not available, it is very important to purchase a fruit and vegetable wash to clean everything you'll be juicing. The wash is usually found alongside the produce, in small or large spray bottles. Using this product will foster the removal of pesticides applied in the growing process. This cleaning step is very important— there are many health risks associated with the ingestion of pesticides.

Always discard bruised or damaged produce before juicing.

You will notice that some fruits and vegetables, such as mangoes, papayas and broccoli don't juice well because they do not contain much water. Also, bananas are better suited for a smoothie in the blender, not for juicing.

DO REMOVE

Moldy, bruised or damaged areas of the fruits or vegetables

Carrot and rhubarb greens—the greens contain toxic substances

Peels of oranges, tangerines, grapefruits, lemons, cucumbers and limes—the peels contain oils that can upset your stomach

Apple cores and seeds, and cherry, plum, peach, apricot and mango pits

DO NOT REMOVE

Beet and radish stems and leaves; strawberry stems—they contain valuable nutrients that are good for the body

Always wash hands thoroughly before handling fruits and vegetables.

Wash all fruits and vegetables before juicing; especially non-organic produce.

Discard bruised or damaged produce.

35

JUICING FOR JOCKS!

JUICING

Recipes

EYE OPENER

TIME OF DAY	Breakfast for any child or athlete.
INGREDIENTS	4–5 carrots 1–2 green apples
BENEFITS	Nourishes, hydrates the body, increases energy & fights fatigue.

HANG IN THERE

TIME OF DAY	In the morning for breakfast or anytime.
INGREDIENTS	5–6 carrots 1 small beet 4–5 leafs of romaine lettuce
BENEFITS	Helps headaches & flushes liver. A headache is a sure sign of dehydration. Promotes liver cleansing from alcohol consumption.

All ingredients listed are per person. Meaning, if you want to make enough juice for two people, double the ingredients; for four people, use four times the amount.

37

HOMEWORK HELPER

TIME OF DAY	After school or before practices or games.
INGREDIENTS	$1/2$ fresh pineapple 1 pear 1 apple
BENEFITS	Hydrates the body, reduces headaches & swelling; energizes.

SWEET SLUSH

TIME OF DAY	After school or before practices or games.
INGREDIENTS	Watermelon only (remove seeds)
BENEFITS	Hydrates & refreshes the body; reduces sweet cravings; flushes out toxins through urinary track.

PRACTICE PUNCH

TIME OF DAY	Before practices or games.
INGREDIENTS	5-6 carrots 2 handfuls of fresh spinach
BENEFITS	Helps constipation, hydrates & nourishes the body, helps with upset stomachs and relieves weakness and dehydration.

RISE N' SHINE

TIME OF DAY	Before or after practices or games.
INGREDIENTS	4–5 Carrots 1 red apple
BENEFITS	Nourishes and hydrates the body; increases energy.

BLOODY GOOD

TIME OF DAY	Before practices or games. Also, take at night to ease breathing and discomfort so you can rest completely.
INGREDIENTS	2–3 small tomatoes $^1/_2$ peeled lemon $^1/_2$ peeled lime 3–4 stalks of celery
BENEFITS	Eases stuffy noses, allergies & headaches. Helps to ease allergy symptoms which can make playing sports difficult.

39

LEAN GREEN

TIME OF DAY	Before or after practices or games.
INGREDIENTS	3–4 stalks of celery 2 handfuls of fresh spinach 1 peeled cucumber
BENEFITS	Calms, energizes, promotes weight loss and eases symptoms of PMS. This juice is good for all sports but especially football and wrestling when weight maintenance is crucial. Replacing a meal with juice before and after practice or games is a way to flush body of excess water weight while still hydrating for energy and endurance.

SWEET TOOTH

TIME OF DAY	Before and after practices and games. Also after dinner, when desert or something sweet is usually craved.
INGREDIENTS	$^1/_2$ whole fresh pineapple 1–2 peeled oranges
BENEFITS	Nourishes, hydrates body & reduces sweet cravings.

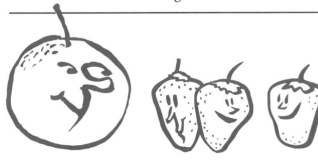

SNOOZE BUTTON

TIME OF DAY	After practice or before bed.
INGREDIENTS	4–5 Carrots 3–4 stalks of celery
BENEFITS	Nourishes, calms & prepares the body for rest. Helps promote sleep.

> Juicing keeps sickness at bay and it breathes life into our bodies on a daily basis.

CARROT COCKTAIL

TIME OF DAY	After a big meal or before bed.
INGREDIENTS	4–5 carrots 3–4 stalks celery 1 peeled cucumber
BENEFITS	Nourishes, helps digestion & will increase energy upon waking.

TROPICAL TWIST

TIME OF DAY	After dinner or before bed.
INGREDIENTS	1–2 peeled oranges 7–8 strawberries $^{1}/_{2}$ fresh pineapple
BENEFITS	Relieves stomach aches, sweet cravings & hydrates the body.

FOOTNOTE:
MUCH OF THE
INFORMATION
ON WHAT THESE
PARTICULAR
JUICES DO FOR
OUR BODIES
WAS FOUND IN:

*The Juice Lady's Guide
to Juicing for Health*
CHERIE CALBOM, MS.,
1999.

OUT GO THE LIGHTS!

TIME OF DAY	Before bed.
INGREDIENTS	4–5 stalks celery 1-2 apples
BENEFITS	Makes sleepy and calms. Wake up refreshed and energized.

add your own favorites!

TITLE:

TIME OF DAY

INGREDIENTS

BENEFITS

TITLE:

TIME OF DAY

INGREDIENTS

BENEFITS

42

TITLE:

TIME OF DAY

INGREDIENTS

BENEFITS

TITLE:

TIME OF DAY

INGREDIENTS

BENEFITS

TITLE:

TIME OF DAY

INGREDIENTS

BENEFITS

Frequently Asked Questions

What is the difference between fresh juicing and the juice that is bought in the store?

The juice that is purchased in the store does not have the benefit of the "live enzymes" which is what feeds the body and gives it nutritional value. Any non-fresh products are void of live enzymes because of the process used to preserve food and extend shelf-life.

Why does the juice have to be drunk within 15 minutes?

The juice needs to be drunk immediately so you get the full benefit of the live enzymes. Your face will look refreshed and your body will feel energized.

Is it possible to make the juice and freeze for later?

You can freeze the juice or place in refrigerator but it is most delicious and nutritious if consumed immediately.

(continued)

Do you usually drink the fresh juice with a meal?

The fresh juice is very filling and can replace a meal so it is unnecessary to drink juice with meals.

Can you engage in active sports after drinking the juice?

Yes. Juicing decreases the risk of dehydration in athletes and sustains high energy and endurance levels.

Is fresh juice easier to digest than store bought juice?

Yes. Fresh juice begins digesting as soon as it enters your mouth. The body does not work as hard at breaking down the juice as it needs to for a cooked meal. Also, there are no chemicals and preservatives to be broken down and stored, so much less energy is used in the process and the body feels stronger and more energized.

Can juicing help you lose or maintain your weight?

Most definitely. Weight loss and weight mainte-nance can be achieved by a routine of daily fresh juicing. You can replace one or two meals a day with juicing and still get all the important vitamins and nutrients in your diet. You will not feel weak or deprived in any way. For more information on weight loss, juice fasting, and detox, please check Chapter 8.

Why is juicing better than eating raw vegetables or cooked vegetables?

Juicing is easier to digest and in its fresh form the body will assimilate nearly 100 percent of the nutrients. When raw fruit and vegetables are eaten whole, the fiber is actually trapped in the food and we are only able to assimilate about 1 percent. Juicing unlocks the nutrients and the body benefits immediately.

How do you get fiber?

Fresh juicing does remove most of the fiber, which makes the juice easier to digest. Also, as a result of juicing, nutrients are available in much larger quantities. Fiber can be gotten from whole fruits and vegetables as well as nuts and grains.

Is juicing safe for people with diabetes and other health problems?

Anyone with health problems should always consult their physician before trying anything new. Talk to your physician and nutritionalist about the benefits of a juicing lifestyle. There are many resources listed in Chapter 8, and a vast amount of information and support which can be found online. Search the Internet for healing diseases, such as diabetes, high blood pressure, obesity, cancer and liver disease with juicing, a diet of raw foods, detoxing and fasting.

If you or a loved one has been sick for a long time and want to explore the possibility of being healthy and strong, then please do some research on the benefits of juicing and raw food. Read or talk to some people that have actually been sick and find out what made a difference for them. It will be worth your time and effort to do this for yourself or for your child.

Juicing is not about treating sickness or the symptoms of sickness—it is about healing the body and *preventing* sickness.

Juicing is not about treating sickness or the symptoms of sickness —it's about healing the body and *preventing* sickness.

FOOTNOTE: INFORMATION AND ANSWERS TO SOME OF THE "FREQUENTLY ASKED QUESTIONS" WERE TAKEN FROM THE FOLLOWING WEB SITES:

WWW.LIVING-FOODS. COM

WWW.NATURETONICS. COM

47

Testimonials

NAME	Joe Gomez
AGE	30
OCCUPATION	Chef

"By the second day of my juice fast, I felt my body and spirit coming together. By the fifth day, my energy level had increased so much that I felt as if my cells were dancing and having a party in my body. As if I were on my way to Oz to find a clean heart, brain, courage and I had killed the wicked witch (those evil toxins) in my body. By the tenth day, I was no longer short of breath and did not need my inhaler. By the fifteenth day, I no longer needed to use my sleep apnea apparatus.

"I believe that juicing can change anyone's life or help improve it. The youth today can benefit from juicing because it helps keep you feeling young and energetic. I feel like I am 18 again.

49

"My inspiration was my family. I want to be here to see my children grow up and to see my grandchildren and even great grandchildren. My son Elijah has cerebral palsy and is a high-spirited child who, despite his inability to walk, crawl and sit up, is so happy and feels he can 'do it'—as he says with everything. I took his energy and said if my son who may not walk on his own can believe he can 'do it' then so can I—and I DID IT. I ran the Chicago Marathon for the first time in my life in October of 2004."

NAME	Carol Roeske
AGE	44
OCCUPATION	Full-time Mom

"We have heard much about different foods through the years but fruits and vegetables have always remained a constant staple when referring to a healthy diet. So, I did not have to think twice about making this a new way of life for me and my family.

"I have been juicing for a very short time but I feel great. I love that I can have carrot, beet, celery, broccoli, apple, spinach and pineapple juice in one glass and have it taste so good. I have also gotten my children involved and to keep them interested in the process, I let them pick out and wash their own fruits and vegetables for their "special" juice. I send family and friends home with samples. Everyone seems to be amazed that it tastes so delicious. The fact that my husband Larry has sampled the different juices is a big deal. He thinks that if he has canned corn with a meal that he has done his body a great service. We are all guilty of poor eating habits at one time or another. Juicing is an opportunity to turn things around and give my children a healthy start each day of their lives. Thanks, Joan, for the inspiration!"

NAME	Eugene Cooney
AGE	40
OCCUPATION	Funeral Home Director

"I was first introduced to the idea of juicing by Joan about four years ago. For several years Joan and Steve treated us to weekends of frolicking in the sun and beach at their summer home with a few other families. One particular morning, which followed a late night, Joan asked me if I would like to try a carrot/apple juice for a heavy head. I laughed and said, 'Very funny, I'll have the usual.' Naturally, that meant a type of juice, but it was from a bottle with spices and accompanied with a shot of vodka, and asparagus used for a straw. I then watched her (double vision) go into her infomercial on the benefits of juicing. I drank the carrot/apple juice just to shut her up and spent the next few hours on the hammock.

"Joan convinced my wife Mary to join in on the raw diet/juicing craze. Mary and I have been in love and married for close to 20 years. Mary and I do everything together. She is a gourmet cook and I am overweight due to the fact. I usually do the slicing and dicing while she sautés, simmers and seasons — all with a bottle or two of wine not for cooking but for the cooks. We used to buy butter by the case and held nothing back on gravy's, fattening sauces, fried foods and desserts. We tried every diet known to mankind. We were successful with the Atkins diet, both losing 40 pounds but I also developed an irregular heartbeat while doing it.

"We purchased a juicer in the summer of 2004. At first, I was turned off with all the fruits and vegetables that she was buying. She would start to preach that they were good for you. Now all my life I was told by my mother that certain things were good for me and that immediately told me that it tasted bad. Mary

51

stopped buying butter and still prepared a gourmet dinner every night. But every morning we started the day with fresh vegetable or fruit juice. It took less time to prepare and clean up than my regular breakfast of bacon and eggs.

"I started to notice a few things as Mary continued on her raw juicing diet. The fridge was nothing to visit for midnight snacks. The goodies disappeared. The fruit bowl that went unused since her bridal shower was filled constantly and the veggie drawer, which usually made a home for my stash of beer, was brimming with of all things vegetables.

"The most significant changes were in Mary. She was a different person. She was upbeat and happy. She was filled with energy. It often took a crane to get her up for work but she was up and about without the use of the snooze alarm. She started making me juice in the morning and she was always in a good mood. (Note to all married men: 'always in a good mood'). She began exercising and cut the booze out of her life. I am more proud of her today than I have ever been. She's a great example for me and my daughter in all aspects of life. I believe juicing with raw foods has had a lot to do with it.

"My daughter, Caitlin, and I have joined in the juicing. Although my diet is not 100 percent raw, I do feel the benefits and nutrition of juicing. I have juice every morning and noon, with a regular meal for dinner. My cholesterol and blood thickness is checked every few months and both have reduced drastically. Even though I am on blood thinners and cholesterol reducing medications, my blood tests have never been so positive. My doctor was very pleased at the dramatic improvement. My wife's health has also improved. Her medical chart could easily be mistaken for an encyclopedia. From head to toe she's had it. Since juicing, everything from her high blood pressure to her sinus problems have gone away. She is an example that shows the benefits of fresh juicing and raw foods."

NAME	Dr. Douglas N Graham
AGE	52
OCCUPATION	Doctor; Author; Advisor to Pro and Olympic Athletes

"In over twenty years of working with professional and world class athletes, I have found that increasing their percentage of fresh whole ripe raw organic plants is one of the key factors in helping them to improve their nutrition, health, and performance. Anyone wishing to instantly feel naturally and healthfully energized and refreshed will benefit by eating more of the only true health foods that exist—fruits and veggies. The elite athletes of the future will likely eat fruits and vegetables to the exclusion of all other foods."

(*To read more from Dr. Graham, please check out his books:* "Nutrition and Athletic Performance"; "Grain Damage"; "The 80/10/10 Diet", *or his Web site:* www.foodnsport.com)

NAME	Christin Stanek
AGE	23
OCCUPATION	Strength and Conditioning Coach

"I did not fight it when my mother shoved that 'Big Gulp' cup of fresh carrot juice in my face at 6 a.m. one day. Although I was too tired to see what I was really drinking, I knew that it was fresh. When you start juicing, your body immediately becomes aware of what is bottled and what is freshly made. It was that 'freshness' that my body started to crave at 6 a.m. every morning.

"I have always been athletic and didn't always adhere to a strict diet of fruits and vegetables. You

53

might say that my diet would definitely be frowned upon by the USDA. My mother always tried to implement a Food Pyramid-recommended item in our diets but none really got our attention like the juicing and raw foods concept. Being a highly active individual requires an intake of a multitude of nutrients, minerals, and enzymes to support the muscular and cellular changes that occur within our system as a result of physical exertion. I needed all this and more growing up and even now to this day. Juicing has alivened by body and awakened my spirit. It has driven me to want more for my health and in turn has created a path of self-discovery. When your body is clear of 'garbage' so is your mind; from there the possibilities for yourself are endless.

"It is interesting how knowledgeable I have become as a result of introducing juicing and raw foods into my life. With the help of my mother, I have learned so much more about the body and how it ticks. Being a health professional I am always looking for avenues of betterment for the body and its health. Since I started juicing and eating raw foods, I have begun to implement their concepts into my training as well as that of my colleagues, clients, and athletes. I have yet to be let down!"

NAME	Katie Gallagher
AGE	30
OCCUPATION	Equities Trader

"Juicing has brought my level of nutritional awareness to an all time high. I will never forget my first juice and how I felt as a result. It was pure good-ness based solely on nutrients and enzymes. My cousin introduced me to my first green juice. It was cucumber, kale, spinach, carrot, tomato, lemon and ginger. I must

54

say at first glance I was a little intimidated. However, I quickly calmed myself, took a sip, drank the whole glass, went back for seconds and never looked backed. What a concept! Think of all the pure natural vitamins and nutrients in just one glass! It would take me days to eat the amount of nutrients which make up one glass of juice. Since juicing removes the fiber, the nutrients are absorbed by the body in much larger quantities than if each vegetable was eaten as a whole.

"I juice throughout my day and have learned to listen when my body craves these fresh, energy-filled drinks. I have done juice fasts for seven days and have never felt better. My energy was boundless, my body was euphoric and an overall positive feeling about myself was present. Kind of like a total body makeover—the natural way! Juicing nurtures the body, mind and soul all at the same time."

NAME	Steven Stanek
AGE	18
OCCUPATION	Student

"Being an athlete and playing football and ice hockey back to back was very intense and it was a challenge to keep my body performing at its fullest capacity. Before I was introduced to juicing, my diet consisted of mostly processed and fast foods. I still considered myself to be in great physical condition considering my young age and my ability to play two very intense sports. My schedule consisted of a full day of school, football practice after school and then ice hockey practice and/or games in the evenings. Meals and homework had to be worked into the evenings as well. It was quite challenging to maintain peak performance in both academics and sports. As soon as I began the juicing routine—something changed for me.

55

"I committed myself to a routine of juicing and realized that it was totally worth it because it was all natural and I could feel the increased energy during the day—especially at practice. The juicing became as routine as taking daily vitamin supplements. I continued to take my vitamins along with the juicing. Juicing definitely makes a difference for athletes and if you combine juicing with healthy eating habits and regular work outs you will see dramatic changes in the way that you feel, look and perform in sports. I really like the fact the juice is all natural. It tastes much better than the store-bought alternatives.

"Juicing is an excellent idea for anyone who is interested in feeling better and being stronger not only in their sport of choice but in their life. Thank you, Mom, for the healthy years ahead of me!"

NAME	Ron Kint
AGE	45
OCCUPATION	Landscape Designer

"I first started juicing when my wife Claudia became pregnant with our 1st son Jack. There wasn't this big dramatic change in either of us, but it just felt right. Jack was born healthy, followed by Adam and then Kees.

"Now with 3 boys, (10, 8 and 4) Claudia and I have a very busy, active life trying to keep up with them. Exercise and eating a balanced diet is key. I like to lead by example, and even though our boys haven't yet adopted the daily fresh juice intake as consistently as I have, I just keep putting it in front of them.

"When you feed your body what it needs, it is going to run more efficiently, and you can do things more effectively. Being in tune with your body is important.

"Juicing for us is a great way to start the day. Hey, don't get me wrong, I still enjoy a few cups of coffee in the morning, but for me it feels good to drink something that I know is going to 'kick start' my day.

"I like a glass first thing in the morning, and then in the late afternoon or evening. Keep it flow'n and keep going! And keep juicing for a healthier lifestyle."

NAME	Tim Raines
AGE	46
OCCUPATION	17-Year Veteran of Professional Baseball

"Being a professional athlete, it has always been important for me to be in prime physical condition, so proper nutrition and exercise have always been a part of my lifestyle. However, when I was diagnosed with Lupus (a chronic inflammatory disease that can affect various parts of the body) in 1999, I became even more aware of my body and its nutritional needs, not just for sport but for long-term health. While analyzing my diet I noticed that I was not eating enough fruits and vegetables, which contain many nutrients and antioxidants essential for good health. Juicing was suggested as a way to increase my intake of natural fruits and vegetables. Since doing so, I have more energy and generally feel much healthier. Now juicing has become a staple of my diet, and I feel much better knowing I'm receiving all the nutritional benefits to help me keep up with my active lifestyle."

57

BOOKS

Detox Your World *by Shazzie*

Dr. Jensen's Guide to Diet and Detoxification
by Dr. Bernard Jensen

Enzyme Nutrition: The Food Enzyme Concept
by Dr. Edward Howell

Feel-Good Food: A Guide to Intuitive Eating
by Susie Miller & Karen Knowler

Lick the Sugar Habit *by Nancy Appleton, PhD*

Lose Weight with Live Foods *by Lani Rossetta, BA, BS*

Juice Fasting & Detoxification *by Steve Meyerowitz*

Raw Family: A True Story of Awakening
by Victoria Boutenko

Raw Kids: Transitioning Children to a Raw Food Diet
by Cheryl Stoycoff

Raw Knowledge: Enhance the Powers of Your Mind,
Body and Soul *by Paul Nison*

Raw Knowledge II: Interviews with Health Achievers
by Paul Nison

RAW: The Uncook Book *by Juliano with Erika Lenkert*

12 Steps to Raw Foods: How to End Your Addiction
to Cooked Foods *by Victoria Boutenko*

The Complete Cancer Cleanse *by Cherie Calbom, MS;
John Calbom, MA; Michael Mahaffey, PC*

The Juice Lady's Guide to Juicing for Health *by Cherie
Calbom, MS*

The Juiceman's Power of Juicing *by Jay Kordich*

The Juicing Book *by Stephen Blauer*

The Raw Life: Becoming Natural in an Unnatural World
by Paul Nison

The Raw Truth: The Art of Preparing Living Foods
by Jeremy A Safron

The Wheatgrass Book *by Ann Wigmore*

Wheatgrass, Natures Finest Medicine
by Steve Meyerowitz

OTHER INTERESTING READING

Medical Madness ...and you are the victim
by Bea E. Sheridan

The Dark Before the Dawn: 70 Secrets to Self-Discovery
by Theresa Castro

The Pleasures and Principles of Partner Yoga
by Elysabeth Williamson (www.wisdom-arts.com)

HEALTH & WELLNESS CENTERS & RESOURCES

Creative Health Institute
112 W. Union City Road, Union City, MI 49094
www.creativehealthinstitute.us

Hippocrates Institute
Palm Springs, FL
www.hippocratesinst.org

Hoffman Institute
www.hoffmaninstitute.com

Karyn's Inner Beauty
1901 N. Halsted, Chicago, IL 60614 — (312) 255-1590
www.karynraw.com

Laura Boynton King, CHT, NLP, Summit Dynamics, LLC
"Imagine Being the Best You Can Be!"
Certified Hypnotist
www.summitdynamics.net

Landmark Education Corporation
www.landmarkeducation.com

Partners in Wellness
1967 N. Dayton, Chicago, IL 60614 — (773) 868-4062
Contact: Alyce M. Sorokie
www.gutwisdom.com

61

JUICING FOR JOCKS!

Conclusion

I hope you've enjoyed my first book and that you have found the information helpful for yourself, your children and your players. I am not a doctor. The information contained in this book is based upon my life experiences acquired over the years in my search to find health, happiness and overall well-being.

You don't have to totally change your eating habits and lifestyle to have health and vitality. Replacing at least one meal per day with live fruits and vegetables can make all the difference in the world.

I would love to hear from you—whether it is comments on the book, questions, family stories or athlete comments. My Web site is www.juicingforjocks.com and my email address is jstanek@juicingforjocks.com.

Have a happy and healthy life and remember— JOCKS RULE!

Love,
Joan Stanek

63

64

ACKNOWLEDGMENTS

I wish to express my sincere gratitude for all the love and support my family and friends gave me while writing *Juicing for Jocks!* They inspired me to write this book and to make a difference in the lives of young children, because the children are the future.

A special thanks to the coaches and classmates of my Landmark Education SELP Class of 2002. It was in their sharing environment that this concept was created. They inspired me on a daily basis.

To Steve, thank you for clearing the space for me to create and finish the work.

To my friends, Stuart Friedman, Leslie Sutphen and Riva Hemond, who shared their time, their ideas and even invested in juicers because they wanted to make a difference in the world. Thank you for your love and support.

To my children, Christin and Steven — you are my heart and I am committed to making a difference in this world for you and your future.

Finally, a very special thank you to my dear friend,

Steven and Christin Stanek

Mary Cooney. Her energy, wit and passion not only brought a smile to my face each day but still continues to warm my heart. Thank you for your love and inspiration—but mostly, for all the belly-busting laughter that we continue to share.

Juicing for Jocks by Joan Stanek only $14.95

WEB SITE ORDERS	www.juicingforjocks.com
EMAIL ORDERS	jstanek@juicingforjocks.com
PHONE ORDERS	(773) 238-8179
FAX ORDERS	(773) 238-2944 *(Please include order form)*
MAIL ORDERS	Juicing for Jocks, LLC. 3400 W. 111th Street, Suite 361 Chicago, Illinois 60655, USA. *(Please include order form)*

BIOGRAPHY

Joan Stanek, founder of **Juicing for Jocks, LLC**, began developing the "Juicing for Jocks" concept in 2002 and incorporated her company in January 2003. The company promotes health education and awareness for young athletes, coaches and parents at the elementary and high school levels.

Ms. Stanek has had an interesting and varied career in several industries, including venture capital, law, real estate development and options trading. In 1998, as a parent of two young athletes, Ms. Stanek became acquainted with —and soon passionate about —nutrition. This lead to becoming an active proponent of juicing and its healing benefits, and sharing her knowledge with family, friends, colleagues... whoever would listen.

Ms. Stanek is now combining her business expertise with her passion. Juicing for Jocks, LLC, is developing health seminars and workshops for elementary and high schools to educate not only the athletes, but also their parents and coaches on the benefits of a juicing lifestyle. *Juicing for Jocks!* is her first book and is being distributed nationally. The target market for the book is athletic associations and programs within grammar school and high schools throughout the 50 states.

Ms. Stanek, 41, grew up in Chicago and has lived in the Midwest all of her life. Currently, she lives in Chicago with her two children. The whole family enjoys a juicing and raw food diet. She is a member of the Illinois Specialty Growers Association, a group that promotes and develops the Illinois specialty crop industry.

ORDER FORM

Juicing for Jocks: copies x $14.95 per copy =		
Sales tax: Please add 8% for books shipped to California addresses.		

Shipping: Please check one:
        ○ By Air: U.S. $4.00 for first book; $2.00 for each additional
        ○ International: $9.00 for first book; $5.00 for each additional
        ○ Special Shipping: Please contact Juicing For Jocks, LLC.		

Total		

PAYMENT OPTIONS

○ Visa   ○ MasterCard   ○ AMEX   ○ Discover   ○ Money Order / Cashier's Check

Card Number

Name on Card   Exp. Date

Signature

SHIPPING ADDRESS

Name   Phone

Address

City   State   Zip

Email

ADDITIONAL INSTRUCTIONS/COMMENTS